Downsizing Made EZ

Stress Less. Live Better.

Ed Zinkiewicz

To Susan and Dennis from Ed & Pat

ACKNOWLEDGMENTS

We gratefully acknowledge the work of movers out there who willingly take charge of people's fond possessions and make sure they get to their intended place without mishap. We also thank the people who take temporary charge of those things that made up our fond memories and find new owners who might also value them.

DEDICATION

We dedicate this book to all those souls who dread the thought of leaving their homes and having to downsize their possessions. Our word to you? Get going. You can do this. Give yourself time. Take small bites. Many, many, small bites. You will get there.

Copyright © 2024 Edward J. Zinkiewicz
All rights reserved.
ISBN: 978-0-9886622-9-2

ABOUT THE AUTHOR

Ed Zinkiewicz developed software applications tailored to business requirements for 40 years. His focus was on the customer: What will best accomplish what the customer needs?

In this book, Ed focuses his skill on the customer yet again. He wants you to have a successful move. What would a successful move look like? For Ed and his wife Crys it meant caring for our environment by avoiding dumping in the landfill. It meant finding homes for everything they cherished. It meant getting to their smaller new home with everything they really needed and only those items they needed and enjoying being there.

Author, speaker, podcaster, and webinar host, Ed has spent the first 12 years of his retirement meeting the challenges and surprises that retirement can bring. He is not an expert in moving. He is not an expert in downsizing. But… he recently moved. And he paid attention. He has collected a wealth of answers and shares what he and his wife learned about moving and freeing themselves from too much stuff.

Along the way they learned how to minimize stress.

WHAT THE PROFESSIONALS SAY

A relevant topic with practical tips in an entertaining read! Ed's storytelling makes what can be a bland subject much more fun. He provides real and doable action items, identifies resources, and makes a daunting task less stressful. I plan to gift this helpful resource to my real estate clients who are facing downsizing, as well as to those who just want to simplify their lives. But first, I'm going to take Ed's advice myself!

Mary Dunn, Realtor/Coach

Downsizing Made EZ: Stress Less. Live Better is more than just a guide to moving—it's a compassionate companion through one of life's most challenging transitions. It addresses the concerns and fears that inevitably arise when contemplating a significant life change. As a financial advisor who knows Ed and Crys personally, I can attest to the authenticity and depth of the insights shared in this book.

Downsizing Made EZ, not only provides a clear pathway and encouragement for starting a new chapter, but also offers lessons and wisdom about life beyond the moving experience. I particularly appreciated the straightforward, experience-based advice, which is both practical and reassuring. The exploration of companies and resources available to assist in this transition, while being environmentally sensitive and fiscally-friendly, is especially useful.

It's a must-read for anyone facing the daunting task of downsizing, offering both support and a blueprint for a successful journey ahead.

As Ed assures us, "You can do this!"

Jerry Moore, Financial Planner

When it's time to think about downsizing or even simply cleaning out old storage areas, a host of emotions get stirred. The sheer size of the effort is often daunting. Adding moving to a different or smaller place makes the whole task seem even more impossible.

With Ed's book, you will be able to prepare for your future and work through the emotions. His guidelines can help you execute the task without fear and with a path to success.

Downsizing Made EZ is now my recommended single resource to help people remove the clutter and frustrations that keep them from discovering new passions, leading extraordinary lives, and sharing their gifts with others so that they can Live WELLthy.

Tempra Mosley, Insurance, Income & Retirement Strategist

Downsizing Made EZ should be required reading for anyone who is, or will be, downsizing. Ed masterfully and systematically takes you through every step, while also addressing some of those pesky feelings that inevitably rise to the surface while going through the process. Also, Ed's stories and pictures throughout the book make it a very enjoyable reading experience. Upon entering the downsizing phase of life, many people don't even know how to start. I will be recommending this book to many of my clients because I can confidently say that, whoever follows the steps and suggestions in this book will be in for a much less stressful and much more organized downsizing experience. All that's required of you is time, desire, and reading THIS BOOK!

Bryan De Cuir, Attorney and Wealth Advisor

CONTENTS

Acknowledgments/Dedication   ii
About the Author   iii
What the Professionals Say   iv
Contents   vi
Foreward   vii

Part 1 Why Did It All Go?   1

    1 Moving Just Looks Easy   3

    2 Why Move   11

    3 The High Cost of Moving   27

    4 Where to Start   41

Part 2 Where Did It All Go?   55

    5 Our Rules for Downsizing   57

    6 Stuff Nobody Wants   61

    7 Stuff Somebody Is Bound to Want   67

    8 Stuff Somebody Took Gladly   73

    9 Useful Guidelines   79

Footnotes and Credits   87

FOREWARD

The thought of downsizing can be overwhelming. It can even block transitioning into a simpler and safer lifestyle. "Rightsizing," as we like to call it, takes thorough planning, determination, and the ability to let go of things not used. All of that has an emotional cost, which is why it is important to make this decision on your own terms, rather than waiting until the choice is no longer yours.

I work with Let's Get Moving! in Nashville, Tennessee. We are a senior move management service accredited through the National Association of Senior and Specialty Move Managers (NASMM). We have helped hundreds of families through this transition, and we know what it takes to be successful in this effort.

Many times, I ask our clients to lean into our process. I guarantee that if they will trust us as the experts, they will be so glad they did. Ed and Crys Zinkiewicz were our clients and a joy to work with. They are a prime example of people who see the value of making this transition earlier rather than later.

Ed has helped many people navigate the issues that come with retirement and aging. He has experienced downsizing and moving firsthand, and he has vast knowledge of how to make this decision, what to expect in the process, and who to turn to for help.

Downsizing Made EZ: Stress Less. Live Better will walk you through many helpful tips, as well as provide you with a healthy knowledge of what to expect. It was an honor to work with the Zinkiewicz family, and I am thankful to be asked to be a very small part of this book.

As you look ahead to your transition, take the content of this book as your survival guide, and then… pun intended… let's get moving!

Connor Glasscock
Business Development Manager for
Let's Get Moving!

Part 1

Why Did It All Go?

1 MOVING JUST LOOKS EASY

Wait Until You See How Much of That Iceberg Is Hidden Under the Water

Whoever said moving was easy was crazy. I mean it looks easy. A big, strong crew comes in, puts all the stuff from drawers into boxes, puts boxes into trucks, transports the boxes, and unpacks the stuff from the boxes, and puts these things back into the drawers they came from. Maybe.

Looks can be deceiving, however.

Why am I talking about moving? Because my wife Crys and I just did.

We moved from our home of 46 years to an apartment in an independent living community. This was a planned move. We didn't have to move, but we thought if there were to be any hope of us knowing anybody there, we ought to make the move while we were still able to get out and meet people.

We discovered that moving is a LOT harder than it looks. Do you know how much stuff you can put into a moderately sized two-bedroom house (with a full attic) in 46 years?

Accumulations of stuff should not be a surprise. When I talk with others about moving or downsizing, they often groan, "Oh, I couldn't possibly do that. I've got too much stuff! Where will I put it all?" These folks recognize the complexity and shear volume just by glancing around their home.

Besides, it's not just about packing, shipping, unpacking. There are three other major steps involved:

- Preparing the house for sale and selling it
- Downsizing and packing
- Remodeling and redecorating the new apartment

Preparing the House for Sale

Who knew there was so much work involved in selling a house!

You can't just invite somebody in to look at your house without sprucing it up a bit. Wash some windows, pressure-wash the deck, fix the latch on the door, a dab of paint here and there, and on.

And on.

And on.

Good grief, Charlie Brown!

When we embarked on this project, our friend Jean said about her move, "We just got the place looking like we want it and then, we left." We felt much the same.

But to sell the house we even had to make it even better. For example, Crys went out to the garden supply and brought some colorful flowers to put in beds around the house so there is a little

color to greet potential buyers or renters in late winter or early spring. Then she spent hours planting, weeding, and mulching. How many bags of mulch does it take to sell a house?

It was January when we heard there was an apartment with our name on it if we wanted it. The kicker? That would make the move date in early June, a mere four months away.

Downsizing and Packing

That's right. We knew about this in January and we're not moving until June. Going to be an interesting school report, "How I Spent My Winter and Spring" by Edward J. Zinkiewicz.

Point of fact we knew we were moving nearly two years ago when we signed up for an apartment. We were number 122 on the list and were told it would take up to five years before we would be offered an apartment.

Surprise, surprise. We got the call in January a scant year and a half later.

During those next months there were many weeks when our living room was like an accordion. Here are the steps:

- Drag stuff down from the attic, out of drawers in the workroom/utility room, hidden in closets, and other mysterious crevices.

- Fill up the couch. Stack more on the chair. Put the extensions in the table to make it longer and fill it up.

- Then, one day it's delivery time; empty it all out. Start over.

Want some storage containers?

Out of curiosity, I started a list two years ago tracking destinations.

- On this day we took an armload to a neighbor who really wanted those things for a charity.

- On another day we filled our SUV to the brim to go elsewhere.

- One Saturday morning I begged my friends at my Toastmasters Club meeting to take upright magazine stands, legal-sized printing paper, padded mailers, and file boxes home with them.

The score? After 90 weeks: 126. We've repeated this process 126 times over a 90-week period or nearly 21 months.

That's three payloads over a two-week period. Did I mention the rate of packing went up the closer we got to moving day?

There was not a day in 21 months when we didn't fill a box, hunt for similar items in hidden crannies, or talk about next steps. The entire process was all consuming in the sense that we were always thinking about it. However, we deliberately paced ourselves. It was only in the last four months that we spent more time each day on actually moving, packing, and deciding.

> Moving does not have to be a frantic effort. My friend Matt Paxton says he "savored the process."[1]

We are the lucky ones. Why? Because we don't have to move everything in the house. Over the course of a week before the movers came, an entrepreneur friend, Paul Radke, bought all the big pieces we didn't want to take (3 couches, 4 arm-chairs, an ottoman, and more) and came by to haul off his loot. A moving company called Let's Get Moving took the majority a few days before we moved in.

That doesn't mean the moving company waited until move-in date. Oh no. The movers came by to put little pieces of blue tape on items that were going or were to be emptied (like closets). They provided a computer-generated layout of furniture in the new place to see what would work and what wouldn't.

How did the computer learn about the layout? We spent days with a little graph paper and small furniture cutouts. Plus, we visited the apartment a couple of times to double-check dimensions.

After 126 trips and more carting and wrapping and packing, the actual move almost seemed a little anticlimactic. Put the remainder in boxes and into the van, unload it and put it where it belongs on the other end. Icing on the cake.

Preparing the New Apartment

Here's the living room in our new apartment three months before the move. Isn't it lovely?

Do you see those boxes on and beside the built-in on the right. Those are our new light fixtures!

The stove sits on the rug at the bottom of the picture, you can see the handle of the refrigerator on the left and a miscellany of items lying about including torn carpet and broken sink stands.

That's what we call progress! At this point the demolition of walls had been done. So, right behind the camera is a gutted kitchen, and the whole place has been gone over to fill nail holes and the like.

At this point in the move, kitchen cabinets had been ordered, we'd selected the countertop covering for the kitchen and bathrooms, added a pair of electrical outlets, picked out the flooring, settled on paint colors, gotten a new door put it, and a wall extended by six inches. The built-in you saw was to be converted to a desk for Crys. The door, wall, and desktop were put in that week!

Excited we were. And not a little impatient.

But there you have it. A little bit of this: The sale and house preparation moved by small steps toward the move date. A little bit of that: The apartment showed signs of being more suited to our needs. And a lot of downsizing: We took a few more steps toward simpler living.

The only problem. All these bits and parts had to be done by a target date. Did I mention that? In late April we found that the early June move-in date had to be moved a week earlier! No pressure.

We were also lucky. Why? Because

- We didn't have to move into temporary quarters while our apartment renovations were being done

- We didn't have a lot of strangers making decisions without consulting us about our cherished things and where they were going to go, or worst yet

- We didn't have to do all of this in one month or less.

Throughout the process we maintained control of where our possessions went. We put a bare minimum in the landfill. We never thought of our stuff as trash, why should it get hauled off as trash. Details follow.

What Did We Learn?

We realized early on that every item in our house had to be reviewed and sent somewhere. We also realized that after 46 years and several contributions from grandparents and parents, there was a LOT of stuff.

What we didn't realize was that to try to sell the house, get an apartment ready, and do all the downsizing at the same time was going to get complicated. For example, we didn't know that selling the house and getting the funds from the sale weren't the same thing.

We were fortunate that selling the house was a five-minute conversation. However, the buyer's ability to get the funding he needed in light of national bank closures added time to the equation. As it turns out, nearly two months.

Our movers, Let's Get Moving, recommended that we split moving and selling. They said that a bridge loan could offset any stress we were facing waiting and hoping closing for the house came in earlier than move-in date when we had to pay our final fee to get into the apartment.

Once we did that, the pressure was off. Of course, we were paying a mortgage and a bridge loan at the same time, but we benefited from the sequential effort.

So, our note to you is to split these things up where you can. There are several arrangements of variables you might consider.

- Downsizing first
- Find a buyer for you house
- Get money from the sale
- Find a new location
- Prepare new home
- Move

You get the idea. Rearrange the moving parts to suit. Having time available is necessary in case of any number of delays possible. And having space to store things temporarily may also be needed.

2 WHY MOVE

Our Story

My wife and I lived in the perfect single-story home, which we thought would go the distance with us. As a bonus, it was only a mile away from our daughter. Why on earth did we ever decide to leave and go through all the hassle of downsizing and moving? Stay tuned. This is our story…

Our Retirement Plan

When we started retirement, we saw ourselves out and about and going. We expected to do things of value that brought us joy. We looked forward to making and keeping up with friends. We planned on staying active. We expected to. We were on an adventure! And adventure we did!

On day one of my retirement, we caught a plane to Boston. We had a lovely time. Even our accommodations were special—a houseboat in the Boston harbor. What a view. The adventure was grand. Just the retirement everybody dreams of. We didn't fill our retirement with travel, but we did have a variety of wonderful trips.

However, on one trip I was struggling to get my luggage off the train when I heard someone behind me yell out, "Somebody help that elderly gentleman." Next thing I knew my suitcase was on the platform and somebody was offering me a hand down the steps.

I was the elderly gentleman?

I do have a little gray hair, so I suppose I've earned that bit about "elderly." But gosh, I don't know what was more disappointing, getting called an elderly gentleman or struggling with a suitcase task that I was able to do easily in the past.

The sad part was that I couldn't get my wife's bag at the same time. I used to haul two suitcases around all the time too.

Unfortunately, it wasn't the first time I'd been caught up short trying to carry something. I remember taking my wife's desktop computer to a technician and wondering how it had gained weight just sitting on her desk. Nobody likes to be frail or be thought of as frail. I had made so much progress in becoming fit, but as the years have progressed, I find a lot of my get up and go has got up and went.

Not completely, of course, but enough to be noticeable. Enough so that I'm curious about the next step. How much harder is it going to be to live in this home we've had for decades? What will be next steps?

As Crys and I discussed our future in retirement, we saw the handwriting on the wall. The older folks we knew were making changes due to aging. The luggage incident was one among many that demonstrated what could be in store for us. So it was that we decided we'd eventually have to move to some kind of retirement facility. We had in mind a place where we would not have as much house and grounds to take care of and, perhaps, not as much cooking and cleaning either.

We had three major concerns:

1. What were some of the dangers ahead? We knew about the strength loss, but we didn't want to ignore other ugly realities that might be waiting. What else might aging have in store for us?

2. We wanted to get a rough idea of how long we had before we needed to move.

3. Finally, we wondered what the warning signs might be. How would we know it was time to jump into that next phase?

I'm going to go through a few of the signs we discovered to give you the thoughts we had along the way.

The Dangers Ahead

I think the biggest one was the chance that some future event might propel us into taking immediate action before we were ready. For example, while we loved our home, we knew we had to get rid of the notion that staying there could last forever.

You've probably heard the stories. Mom broke her hip and had to go to the hospital. Dad's heart attack means changes ahead. Mom can't see any more. Dad can't hear any more.

When these things happen, where will you move to? Have you reserved a spot? Do you need to reserve a spot?

One of the big things right now that had us worried was our stuff. For example, how do you get rid of a house full of possessions right now? They just won't disappear that quickly.

Another one of the big things we were concerned about was what happens when the hospital stay is over and the nurse shows up. We can go ahead and pop into the wheel chair. Then we get to go someplace where you can get care. Do you have a plan for that? Do you have a place for that?

All these questions come up again if you have a limited physical rehabilitation stay. Eventually, you get strong enough to go home. Will you be strong enough to live there with your spouse or perhaps without your spouse? Will you need assistance? Where will you go? Will the place you want to go have room when you need it? Can you find someone to care for you on short notice? What's the plan?

It's one thing to want to live out all your days and then die in your own bed at home. It's another if a loved one (or two or three) will have to pick up the loose ends. Even if hospice is involved, it takes other caregivers to see that meals are prepared, rooms cleaned, and

activities of daily living are under control. That often means a spouse or an adult child must be around.

A good friend of ours recently spent an entire year taking care of these details when her husband was under hospice care in their home. Fortunately, two of their adult children were able to come each at different times to help. One was a nurse and the other experienced with in-home, long-term care. Our friend said she could not have managed without their help. Someone needs to care for the caregiver!

What level of care could you undertake? Are you willing to help your loved one bathe, get dressed, and get on and off the toilet? How do you feel about cleaning their genitals, transferring them in or out of the bed to a chair, changing diapers, or helping them eat?

The experts talk about Activities of Daily Living or ADLs.

- Bathing
- Dressing
- Toileting
- Transferring
- Continence
- Feeding

As your ability to do these things erodes, your need for assistance grows. The sequence starts when you need meals brought in regularly. It can escalate to needing someone to "cut up the meat." Tomorrow you may need someone to feed you.

In other words, you may not get "well" when these things start to deteriorate, and you'll need more assistance rather than less. These problems also often travel in tandem. If you need help bathing, chances are you'll need help transferring from bed to chair or getting up to walk.

While the Activities of Daily Living (ADLs) are important, there are conditions. You are in mortal peril if you can't get out of bed and out the door when there is a fire. Some assisted living facilities may not even admit you if you can't do that on your own.

My wife and I started talking about what needs to happen when we reached these milestones. We also started to assess what support might come from our daughter and family. We didn't want our daughter to feel like she would be stuck. After all, she has a life and career and her family. We cherished those things for her. We certainly didn't want to feel she was obligated to be the only support for her mom and me should we need it.

Is It Time To Give Up Those Keys?

If you live long enough, you will very likely need to stop driving. What are you going to do when you can no longer drive? Will you have groceries delivered? How will you get to and from the doctor's office? What about spending time with friends or going to worship?

I'm sure you've heard people say, "I'm never giving up my car." Or "You can have my car keys over my dead body."

These people are not only resistant, but they are also persistent and stubborn about it. I also know someone who hid that fact that she had had several small accidents. She got away with hiding the details all the way up to the last accident, which injured someone else. Permanently!

Are you going to wait for another accident? What are the warning signs that it's time to turn those keys in? What will you do?

You get the idea. Crys and I realized our future needed provisions for transportation, reduced care of house and grounds, help with cleaning and at least some meals. It would be icing on the cake if we could also have rehabilitation care, assisted living, and long-term health care.

Wow. We had our work cut out.

> Downsizing to a simpler life can be a safety measure.

How Long Do We Have?

Of course, the next question was going to be how long do we have? When will we have to execute our plans. There is no way to pick a number with any certainty. Anything could interrupt the best plan or make new plans necessary.

Despite all that, there is a deadline! Wherever we ended up, we wanted to be able to get out and still do. We wanted to meet some new folks and enter new relationships. We wanted a buffer against being alone.

And we wanted some help in meeting whatever the new challenges were going to be. For example, if we couldn't lift much, we wanted to do what we could to get stronger. For me that meant hiring a trainer.

We also realized the need for the support of a group and the discipline of a schedule for exercising. We wanted to push the limits on what we could do physically to stay as fit as circumstance permitted.

So, not really knowing, we took a wild guess at 20 years or so. We were in our early 60s when these discussions began, and we struggled to pin-point a date, so we said "around the age 85" we'd likely make a move. Setting a date like this is more an art than it is a science, but what we saw was that people between 80 and 85 often needed to make a change.

Most of the folks we knew in the previous generation made some kind of downsizing move around that time. Even my mom moved to an apartment that was smaller at that point in her life. I had thought she was rooted in that house for life!

What Are the Warning Signs?

This question was even more difficult: What are the indications that you're ready or need to move? When will you become a candidate to leave your home?

I am going to drill down into the when question right now. Here is what the transition looked like for us.

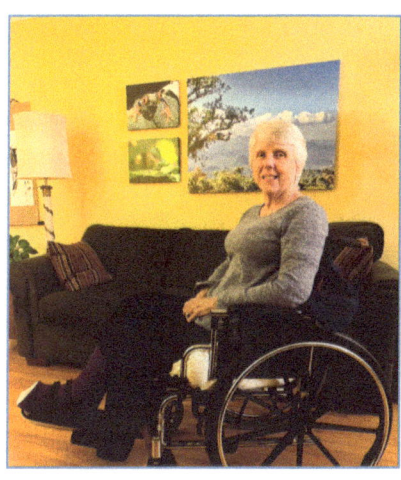
We had our first clear sign when my wife Crys broke her ankle.

This happened January 2, 2020. We were in Costa Rica. The travel insurance company assigned a nice lady who spoke Spanish to help us with the transition. On travel day she literally got Crys out of our hotel room in Costa Rica and put Crys to bed in our own bedroom at home late that night. She had planned the entire trip and stayed with us the whole way.

It was an interesting trip getting Crys home. Did you know there were very narrow wheelchairs that could go down the aisle in an airplane? I stood on the concourse of the Atlanta airport watching our assigned caregiver take Crys to the ladies' room. I said to myself, "How would you have managed to do that?" I was so grateful that we had help.

It was in the days that followed that I discovered that loss of strength was going to make a big difference.

When we were doing our planning after retirement, we were completely satisfied with our house. We judged that no move was necessary and wouldn't be for some time. It was a single-level ranch-style house.

We were happy with that because it meant we could stay in the house longer than some people who might not be able to navigate the hill the house was on, stairs between floors, or split-level ups and downs. We didn't have a staircase or any of those other things that mandated going up and down. We improved things by removing carpets that we could trip on, providing a walk-in shower with weight-bearing appliances like towel racks, and making other improvements to avoid known hazards to seniors.

There was one little flaw in that plan. Access to the house meant getting up to the porch and from the porch into the front door. Just two modest steps. The interior was on one level with navigating only two steps. Piece of cake. Right?

When we were planning, we hadn't counted on not being able to get someone in a wheelchair up and down those two steps! In 2020 I could no longer manage those steps pushing or pulling a wheelchair with a wife in it. I thought I could do it. But I also thought about what might happen if I lost control and dumped her onto the icy, snowy ground. I was not confident in my ability. Suddenly our ideas that this house could "last us forever" took a hit. Even small impediments could become full-blown obstacles.

Luckily our neighbor worked from home and was able to help us with those ups and downs to get Crys to and from the doctor—literally our only excuse for Crys to leave the house for those months of recovery.

During those long 10 weeks we learned some valuable lessons. We learned a little of what it meant to be helpless. You can't do for yourself. We also learned what it meant to be helpful—24/7. Particularly at the beginning, Crys could not dress herself, wash herself, or bathe and could only offer a little support to the multitude of daily chores: cooking, cleaning, grocery shopping. We watched while all these things transformed her emotions to include feelings of dependence.

We also learned a little about the caregiving side of things. A caregiver's life is also transformed.

- Supporting the spouse emotionally.
- Doing the many things she used to do herself.
- Plus trying to keep up with one's own routines and responsibilities.

Caregivers can lose their own sense of independence.

Here's a tip for you. During these excursions into caregiving, make notes. How does it feel to lose your independence? Is caregiving of any interest to you for the long haul?

Sadly, after 2 1/2 months with Crys confined to a wheelchair, we rolled into another level of confinement thanks to the pandemic. COVID19 was ravaging the country. At the time isolation seemed to be our only safeguard. Mandated isolation happened almost immediately after Crys began to walk again. We got her out of the house and into church exactly once in 2020. Like the rest of the country, we settled into a routine of Zoom meetings, a lot of TV shows and live-stream broadcasts, and little else.

Isolation was compounded by inactivity. There was a constant stream of questions about how we could spend our time. Puzzles helped. Double solitaire got old.

My second tip for you is to take seriously the questions of how well you will meet the challenges of isolation. You don't need a pandemic to feel the effects either. Aging-in-place has isolation as a major drawback.

We were fortunate. We had each other. But we also had friends who had no one to turn to and consequently were in much worse shape.

We could visit our daughter, son-in-law, and grandson. We stood on their front lawn and sang the birthday song.

But isolation was the norm.

We were fortunate. Our daughter and her family lived close by. While the weather was good and even after it became necessary to wear coats, we met on our deck. Her family on one side. My sister at the end. Crys and I on the other side. We maintained the social distancing that was recommended, and the long months wore on.

What could you do if your family were not near?

The other saving grace was Zoom and other networking programs. I was able to get to Toastmasters' meetings via Zoom, and we still meet hybrid on Zoom today. During COVID we opened the club to members from other states because we were no longer limited geographically. Today, we still have the option to live-stream worship and attend Sunday School because of the experimentation that started in 2020.

Not everyone had access to computers or decks or even family. They were alone.

COVID exposed the real meaning of isolation. That was our second clear sign.

Remember 2021? We thought COVID was over, but it was not.

Luckily, halfway through 2021 we got a mental reprieve. We were chatting with our friends Jean and Chuck, and they said they were looking forward to soon being able to move into a very nice retirement community called Richland Place.

They said "Most of our friends from our Sunday school class are there already. You should come to. We'll have a blast." Wow. What a call to action.

If we wanted to do that, however, we needed to act quickly because Richland Place had a 4–5 year waiting list, and we needed to get on soon. Chuck and Jean had already been on the list for 3 years and were looking forward to moving in the next year or so, give or take.

Crys and I did some mental calculations. Remember that 80–85-year range we had discussed? At the time Jean and Chuck extended the invitation I was 76 and Crys was 75. Add five years and it seemed to us that by then it might be time.

Crys is an avid gardener. Our backyard had multiple active garden areas with different arrangements that she had lovingly built and tended. And that was just in the backyard. She didn't feel any need to give them up. She was able. She was fit. She loved doing it.

However, she realized that she wasn't going as fast or as far as she used to. She figured that she might be more ready in the next five years.

So, off we went to check Richland Place out. This picture shows our apartment's balcony. I don't know if having a chance to create a new garden like this was the final selling point for Crys. If it wasn't, then this pool was!

Crys loves swimming, and the availability of a pool would give her a chance to swim laps more often.

The apartments were fine too. We signed up on the spot and plunked down our deposit.

Making a decision of this magnitude without discussing pros and cons first and, in particular, not discussing options with our daughter was a departure from the norm in our household. But doing so made our whole quest a little more real. Soon after, we did talk to our financial advisor and yes, for a reality check, we did talk to our daughter and family, who were both supportive and relieved.

The clincher came at the beginning of 2022.

I had my hip replaced. After six to nine months of growing hip pain and a series of treatments that had limited success, the doctor suggested that I was a candidate for hip replacement. So, on January 10 of 2022, I had the joint replaced.

Don't be alarmed. I was asleep the whole time. One minute the anesthesia assistant was asking me if I was ready to get this done and

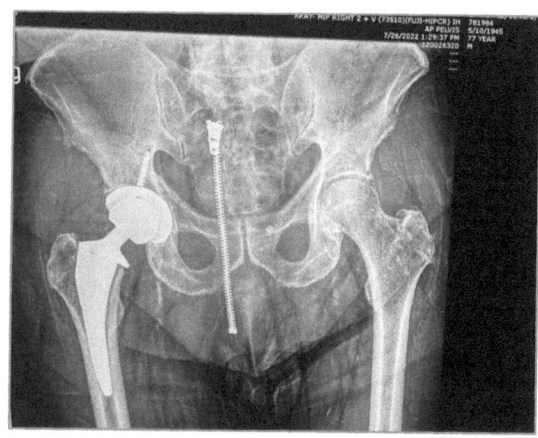

the next thing I remember was the same nurse asking me if I was in any pain. Boom. It seemed just that quick to me. And, yes, I was in pain.

It amazes me that I have a titanium part. Be assured: the zipper was not installed.

Of course, there was a recovery period, and I didn't really get back to going full speed for six months. But most of the pain was gone!

During this time Crys and I traded places. Crys found out what it meant to help me get dressed, put ice packs on for 20 minutes out of every two hours, and assist me with rehab exercises that were never easy and often painful.

Gradually, day by day things got better.

Her earlier observation was confirmed: Being a caregiver, you get to find out what it means to do your own stuff, do your spouse's stuff, and help with rehab. It's demanding and tiring.

What Did We Learn?

The prospect of moving to a retirement community was looking better and better.

We had a whole list of what we considered positive outcomes from picking Richland Place as our next home. One of our biggest concerns had to do with long term health care. The place we chose has a rehab center as well as assisted living center with skilled nursing available. As residents in the independent living area, we would automatically go to the head of the line if assisted living or nursing care were mandated. The availability of these services is a comfort against our anxieties about caring for each other.

In addition to regularly scheduled van service to the grocery, we can also count on scheduling rides for things like doctor's appointments. When the time comes to give up those keys, our transportation needs will likely be covered.

Combine all those ingredients, and it appeared as though all our ducks were in the proverbial row.

We were ready for a change.

We felt a need to take steps to assure the availability of an increased level of care for us as we age.

We found and were beginning to look forward to a new adventure.

That'll be fun.

All we had to do was find a new home for all the stuff we had accumulated in the house we'd lived in for 46 years.

3 THE HIGH COST OF MOVING

Before you start moving, I want you to calculate the cost. There is a very high cost to moving. Everybody knows it costs a lot to get movers, but hiring movers is only the start. When they pack and unpack for you, the cost goes up.

If you don't want movers or that expense, you not only get to pay a lot of money to rent a truck, but also you get to put in the labor. If you don't want to rent a truck, you may be able to use sweat equity alone. The most expensive move I ever made was across the street. No planning, no boxes, no nothin'. Take those three books over there. Rinse. Repeat. Rinse. Repeat. Ad nauseam. Took forever. I don't advise that. But there you have it. Your expense to move could be in money or in time. You're going to pay one or the other or both.

If that were not enough, there are other expenses as well, often secreted away under the hood. They aren't talked about much. One of them, I think, is stress.

Stress Is One, Large Hidden Cost

Stress comes from the usual places: deadlines, costs, unknowns, surprises.

As a start, think of all the questions involved. Can I move from my home of nearly a half a century to a new place? Really? Can I get it all done in time? Can I afford all the costs including the labor? Have our plans covered all the options we need to deal with? Will we get a buyer for our house? Will we get enough money for the house to be able to do this move at all?

Let's start with deadlines. We had a retirement community selected. The apartment we picked would not be available until a certain date. In our case it would be about four months off. To afford the move, we needed to sell our house. We felt good about finding a buyer as someone spoke up early in the game. Could they raise the money in time? Could they afford what we needed? There were several unknowns.

About six weeks into the four months, it turned out that buyer would not be able to make the purchase. The stress-filled reality of "surprise" raised its ugly head. We had to start over and reach an even tighter deadline.

The same kind of thing happened about two months into the four. We had a date we'd been talking about for at least two months when the moving company said they couldn't do that date. They either could do it a month later or ten days earlier.

Adding on a month would change entirely too many other scheduled activities like the date our old couches were disappearing and the date the new couch was to come.

We sped things up. Again. More stress.

During the two years prior to the move, we had a huge mismatch to resolve. Our new apartment was much smaller than our old home. Where was all the stuff going to go? And some of the furniture we might have taken just wouldn't fit. What other things were going to be needed that we didn't have?

We seemed to be immersed in a whole new level of unknowns. What will we need to take, purchase, give away, or sell?

Before we made the actual move, we had a year and a half to figure out some of the answers. The deadline just upped the ante on how quickly things had to be done and, consequently, on our stress level.

To give you some idea, before we knew the date, we took 100 sets of things out of our house. A set of things included everything that went to one place on one day.

Here is a picture of our two cats. Finding a home for them was QUITE A CHORE. They are both outside cats. Where we were moving, we could take pets, but only indoor varieties. These two did NOT fit in that mold. You see them here, resting up so they could go out and spend the night terrorizing the chipmunk population.

We were lucky. We found a farm owner who loved animals, already had a collection of dogs, cats, goats, and more, and was willing to take our animals. Getting them there?

The High Cost of Moving.

Oh, boy. That was fun. We ended up taking these two separately. Each delivery constituted one trip.

We also took a variety of cat items to a friend for their cats. Kitty litter, litter pan, flea combs, cat food, and cat pan liners. Another trip.

Here you see laid out on a picnic table the items included in what my wife called her "horsey gear." Crys was an avid horseback rider for 50 years. This mound included a saddle, tack, toolboxes for hauling tack, pictures, books, jewelry, and, as you can see, even a waste can.

Over a period of 18 months, we did 100 of these trips. In the four months from when we had a hard move-in date until we moved, we made another 70 trips.

The more decisions we had to make on one day, the higher the stress built up.

The Biggest Hidden Cost May Be LOSS

Some people avoid loss. They don't want to get rid of their home, for example. They don't want to get rid of their possessions. They don't want to get rid of these things that they've cherished or that they've spent so much time earning and getting. It's very hard on them when a move is necessary.

I'll illustrate.

In 1977 we invested in a modest three bedroom ranch-style house. 46 years later we didn't leave that house. No.

The house we left had a total makeover complete with the front porch, bay window, and the driveway that you see here. In that time, we also remodeled the kitchen, added a deck, took out a brick wall in the den overlooking that deck and put in a 4-panel glass French door. Here is the house we left.

Then there are the dozen or so garden areas that my wife improved, new paint (several times), new roofs, an upgraded HVAC system, remodeled bathroom (twice), and total water supply and electrical wiring replacements.

We poured equity into this house. And we poured attention and planning and LIFE into this location. 46 years' worth. My wife and I grew up (figuratively speaking) in this house, we raised a daughter in this house, and we helped raise a grandson in this house. We spent our careers in this house and the first decade of our retirement. Moving was going to be a big LOSS.

What about you? Are you heavily invested in where you live? Will you miss it should you leave? Do you have memories that are tied to the location: "I kissed your mom for the first time under that tree right over there."

The problem is the reasons to have to move don't go away. You sometimes can't get your mobility back. Many can't avoid needing care. And sometimes the old homestead is a constant, unwanted source of memories: "I can't wait to get out of here. I kissed your mom for the first time under that tree right over there. Now that she's no longer here, I hate all these reminders popping up all day, every day."

Faced with having to move, how will you do it?

In my experience and from reading I've found there are three general approaches to undertake leaving your home. Each has its own kind of costs. All three involve downsizing. All three involve packing and unpacking. But how they are done can make a big difference.

Before we get started, take out a blank piece of paper. At the top, put a title "My List of Acquaintances." You'll want to leave room to put names and contact details for people you know.

You will use this paper to identify all the people you know who are of an age that they could or have downsized their home and/or have moved.

The goal is to end up with a list that will be a resource to you as you consider options. The closer you are to the people on the list the more likely the list will be helpful.

Go ahead stop reading to get started. Create your list. Keep it handy; you will need it as we go along.

One and Done

The first type of loss I call the BIG LOSS. It can be characterized by speed. These moves are often "One and done."

Loss is THE single word that describes a great deal of what happens to all of us. You probably have lost friends, jobs, bets, weight, arguments, and on and on.

That's not to say that anyone must wait until they are "OLD" to experience loss. By no means. Loss is somewhat of a constant for everyone. But as you grow older, the losses seem to get more serious. Without a car, you realize how much of your life is tied up in getting where you wanted to go whenever you chose. It's a loss of independence.

When you move from a beloved homestead, you seem to leave behind more than you can find elsewhere. You're not going to look at that tree in front of your new house in the same way you looked at that tree where you "kissed your wife for the first time" or pushed the swing you hung for your daughter. The backyard won't have the same gardens that you tended to perfection.

Now imagine if you give up these things all at once, and you will be imagining what I call the BIG LOSS.

I encountered the BIG LOSS the first time with my mom.

Mom sent me a letter. She intended to sell the family home and invited me to attend the auction. All the possessions that weren't sold to "special buyers" picked by the auctioneer were to be sold to the highest bidder. She had hired an estate-sales company.

Mind you, this was the house where I spent most of my life until I left for college. I guess I should have seen this coming. My daughter and son-in-law came back from a trip to mom's a month before the auction and surprised me with the announcement, "Gramma is moving to an apartment." The house sale provided an end-cap for her move.

But the letter was a surprise. She hadn't involved us in the decision about moving. At all. So, of course, I was curious and empathetic for her big move. If she wanted me involved at this point, I wanted to be there.

The sale took all day. She had hundreds of items arrayed in the house, in the garage, and on the lawn. The auctioneer went from one to the next and careful records were made and the final sales made off to one side.

On toward the end of the event my mom said, "There goes all my pretty stuff." In a single day she sold most of her life's accumulation of household goods.

She was saying goodbye to a whole lifetime. "There goes all my pretty stuff."

In one event. In one day. That made the loss a big deal. You get the picture. My mother was embarking on what you and I would call downsizing.

And, she hadn't counted on the hard stuff, the feelings of loss. I don't particularly think she felt regret. But I do think she had not counted on feeling anything at all. The loss was a surprise. Watching reminders of her life disappear piece by piece over the course of one very long day was a stark reveal.

The actual downsizing took more than a day. But the entire transition was brief. Very brief. So it was, she had turned her life from house to apartment in two steps. Only two.

I have no idea how much preplanning went into this move. Knowing my mom, it was probably quite a lot. She had nothing left in the estate sale that she was claiming. All that she wanted to keep she had already moved.

Mom had moved the essentials and her favorites to settle into a two-bedroom place just blocks away from her favorite bingo game. But still. All her stuff in one month? She'd lived there over 50 years. It was a lot to say goodbye to all at once. It was a BIG LOSS.

Let's go back to the list of people you have started. Add some notes of who on that list did just what my mother did—move in a very short time.

Spend some time with these folks. Show curiosity. Was there a particular reason they had to move? Why did they do it in such a short period of time? How do they talk about the experience now?

These reasons are varied and important. You will find in them a wide range of motivations for these dramatic changes. Some you may not have thought about before. This exercise is mental preparation for what might come.

I have heard many stories: Dad can't get to the only bathroom on the second floor anymore. We must move now!

I heard of Mary. Mary went into rehab. Her son was very gracious about it. Put her in a rehab that was close to him so he could be nearby. When she got out of rehab, she was put in an assisted living, also near where he lived because he wanted to make sure that that she was cared for. It sounds good until you find out that he sold her house, and he sold all her possessions, and he picked out where she was going to live—what she would take—all without talking to her.

Big Loss.

As you discover each story, turn it over in your mind. Do you relate to that? Does that look like your situation?

These moves can be by your own volition or not, but they can be hard on you because they happen all at once.

Rinse and Repeat

There are other alternatives to the BIG loss.

My wife's Aunt Lois offers an excellent illustration. Aunt Lois sold her house where she and her husband had raised six daughters. She moved to a two-bedroom condominium. A couple of years later she moved to a one-bedroom apartment. More time passed and she moved to a studio apartment. She ended her days at her daughter's house in a bedroom with bath that her daughter had provided for her.

I call these moves "Rinse and Repeat."

These moves happened over the course of many years, well over a decade. You can think of this plan as a series of LITTLE LOSSES. It was a very gracious, gradual, long-term approach.

She downsized gradually. Sometimes we were on the receiving end. She had shelves set aside for stuff. "Take what you want." Her husband and I had shared a love of storytelling. I received a little figurine of a storyteller in action to remind me of him and our connection. Aunt Lois? She said goodbye gradually. And she had time to gift what she wanted to and to donate what she could.

She treated each move as a compartment. This time I'm donating these things. This time I'm selling these things. This time I'm giving up these things.

She had time enough to remember how special this item was and how important that picture was, but at the same time she had a lot left to cherish.

With this way of managing loss, if there is grieving involved, it is only about a limited set of possessions at any one time.

She wasn't worried about everything all at once.

The High Cost of Moving.

Let's go back to the list of people you made. Make some more notes of who on that list did just what Aunt Lois did.

After class do some homework. Was there a particular reason people on your list had to move? Disadvantages/advantages? Was there a particular reason they did it that way? How do they feel about their experiences

Find New Homes

My wife and I offer a third method. We were concerned to find homes for our stuff where these things could be valued.

By and large when things left our house, they were going someplace where they would be of benefit. So, for example, we gave collections of stuff like coins and stamps to collectors. Sets of silver went to refugees who were starting their lives over, horseback riding gear went to a facility that was supporting battered children, and depression glass serving dishes went to our daughter and the place settings went to a friend who wanted to use them. A large collection of Egyptian art including papyrus paintings went to an Egyptian art fan.

An eclectic set of things were sold to an entrepreneur who would resell them. We didn't know who would end up with these items, but we knew they had some value because we were sure our entrepreneur wanted to come out ahead on the transaction.

Another advantage to us was that the entrepreneur did all the transporting. He also did it on a schedule coordinated with our move.

Several carloads of stuff like lamps and book ends went to a local thrift shop where buyers could acquire needed furnishings at reasonable prices.

Then there was the standard destination called Goodwill Industries and a local place called Turnip Green Creative Reuse. Goodwill took things like towels and linens while Turnip Green took office supplies like scotch tape, pencils, folders, pads, and lots more.

Among the hardest things we had to reduce were letters. My wife inherited a great pile of letters that her mother, a schoolteacher, received from past students. Decades worth. Probably not worth keeping but at the same time reading the letters has illuminated a lot about my mother-in-law and her relationship with a host of people who were important to her. In getting rid of that big box, Crys has gained more clarity about her family and the values she learned from them.

We didn't count recycling. You can reasonably assume that once pictures were made of the letters and photos we wanted to keep, they got recycled to be reclaimed by nature.

How is your list coming? Did you see any commonality between what Crys and I did and what some of your friends have done?

You can take away a lot from this chapter if you put yourself mentally in these strategies and then take measure of your comfort level.

What Did We Learn?

Our method was like my mother's but without the urgency. We got rid of everything in one move. But it took two years to do. On the other hand, we were only evaluating a small portion of items at a time. The 170 trips took two years. Like Aunt Lois, we had considerably less to lose in each trip.

We also had a chance to say, "Not this time." If we found something we weren't quite ready to part with, we could hold on to it and evaluate it again later. There were plenty of opportunities to say goodbye when we were more ready.

Where will you land? Do you want to move quickly or take your time?

Do you really want to have your kids inherit the job of figuring out where everything will go?

Are there items you'd be willing to part with now?

Do you want to be caught up short and have to move in a hurry?

What plans have you made about next steps? Where will you go?

I tell people that retirement is an adventure. These decisions are trail markers on that path. Have fun and good luck.

> Loss is inevitable. You can decide how much of it you endure at any one time.

4 WHERE TO START

Our preparation for the move started by scouting out the territory. We wanted to know as much about where we were going as possible so we could make better choices about what to take. The more you know the better off you are.

Luckily for us, the place we were moving to was only a mile away. We could visit. And we did. Often. We wanted a feel for how much room there actually was. We kept a measuring tape ready to hand.

We have friends who moved several hundred miles to be closer to their son. They did not have the luxury of knowing where they were going or what it looked like firsthand. Luckily their son got involved in the house-hunting and the move preparation. My friend said, "He sent us about a thousand pictures."

Maybe not the best preparation for a big move, but then, they didn't have to worry much about downsizing.

Preparing to downsize involves careful planning. We did two things to begin that process.

We started with a floor-plan. We then drew a scale model and put our measuring tape to work to get exact details including the location of electrical outlets.

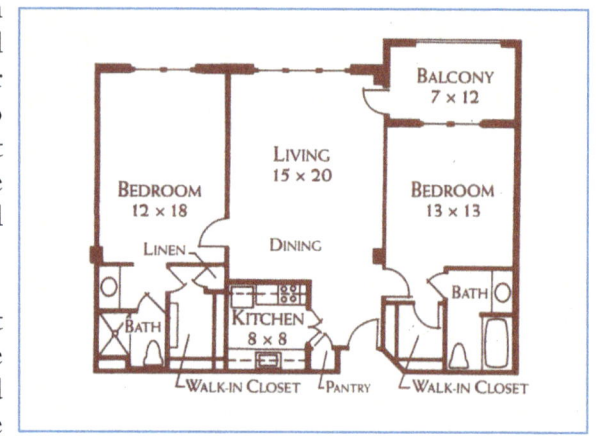

We realized that much of the furniture we had would not make the move. There just was not room for 3 couches, 4 stuffed chairs, and an ottoman. They were too big.

Our next step was to inventory what we had. We included such things as end tables but did not include details about what was in or on the end table. We essentially listed every large item and took care to include measurements and location. For example, we had a five-and-a-half-foot buffet (66 inches) in the dining room. As you can see, we planned to relocate that into the living room in the new apartment.

The Key Questions

Our son-in-law made a helpful contribution at this point. He asked key questions, **"How do you spend your time? What does your world look like? Just how do you 'live' at home now?"** Thinking about that made several decisions very easy.

As my wife loved to garden, she could use the balcony as a container garden to enjoy. We and our new friends have appreciated what she's done on our balcony.

Using those key questions, we realized we didn't need a big space for watching TV. Consequently, we purchased a new, smaller couch and placed it across the room from our TV so we can watch a show.

We have a long tradition of weekly family dinners, so having chairs and table were a must. My wife and I are both writers, so two office spaces were needed. You get the idea.

Besides, making plans to go to a place where we could do what we liked to do only improved our chances of making the move without feeling a great deal of loss. Going to the new place would feel like going home; it would have space for our favorites. We could look forward to those "living spaces" and not feel as though we'd lost things.

Our next step? Arrange furniture in our new apartment. Working with the major ideas we garnered about what we like to do, we started planning.

From the age of ten, our daughter loved drawing room plans on graph paper. As soon as she saw that lovely floor plan, she whisked it away and the next day brought back detailed graph paper layouts with stiff-paper cutouts for the furniture pieces. We had several go-rounds with this design all the while paying attention to our son-in-law's advice.

Description	Dimensions	Current	Future
Dining Table	44x44x40	DR	LR
Buffet	19x66x31	DR	LR
6 Dining Chairs	20x18x38	DR	LR
1 Drawer Side Table	15x22x22	LR	LR

We took these layouts to the apartment and began stepping off placement and checking numbers with the measuring tape. We were asking questions like, "If we put piece here, it will extend out to here. Does that work?"

We also had surprises. "Whose bright idea was it to put support pillars in those corners?" Yep. There were floor to ceiling posts (13 inches by 5 inches) in opposing corners in the bedroom that were not on the layout we were given. That messed up the initial furniture arrangement a bit.

Despite surprises, we had a good idea of what pieces of furniture were going and what we would not keep. This happened early in the process. Our next step was to plan what "stuff" was going that would fit in or on that furniture. Clearly, we had to downsize.

When to Start Downsizing and How

We could not take everything that we owned with us. That was our excuse for getting rid of things. There are other good reasons.

> Planning on what you want to do moves the focus from what to do with things to how you want to spend your life.

1) **Do you have a room in your house you can no longer comfortably get into?**

Having a room like that is a good excuse to downsize in and of itself. Our so-called back room was not quite as bad as the room in the picture but, like most families, it was the room where we put things we didn't have a good place for. These items didn't "belong" there; we just didn't want to see them elsewhere in the house.

Here is why having a clutter room is dangerous: If you can't get in there, you forget what's there. If you forget what's there, you may just buy another. If you buy another, where will it go? The danger with clutter rests in that it is often the root of more clutter. Care to guess how many boxes of paper clips and staples and rubber bands my wife and I had in our desks and our supply cabinets?

2) **How many toasters do you really need?**

Not only might you have duplicates, you may have one too many. Do you use that fancy mixer you bought years ago? We thought it was a great idea when we got it. Turned out to be a dust collector.

3) **What will you do with all that precious art your daughter made in her preschool now that her son is in college?**

We had an attic replete with precious, memorable items. What were we to do about those?

4) **What is all that stuff?**

After living in our house for 46 years, we accumulated a lot of mystery boxes. A portion was family memorabilia that we inherited. Another portion turned out to be just empty boxes stored against the time we might have to carry something out of the house.

Clearing out the clutter, ridding yourself of duplicates, caring for all those sentimental keepsakes, and identifying all those mystery accumulations provide some of your challenges ahead.

Tackle these problems before they start to gang up on you. You likely have space in your home you can't use, items you find yourself working around or having to dust, and mounds of boxes containing who knows what that you don't need or care to have any more. Start there.

At the very least, these are worries you don't need. Left to flourish, this lack of control leads to stress.

Let's talk about how you might make some headway against the headwinds.

Any of these four avenues—clutter, duplicates, passions, mysteries—are good starting places. I've heard a lot of people give up on need to downsize because they don't know where to begin. The easy answer is that you can **start anywhere**. The more practical answer is to pick something and focus on that.

It is more important to get started than starting with the right thing. The big secret about moving is that you're going to have to view, touch, decide, and move everything in your house. Particularly at the beginning, I encourage you to get going. Besides, getting started and doing something is progress, and progress itself is a good motivator.

If you reach a dead end, you can tackle a different spot. Don't lose momentum. Today is a downsizing day. Don't stop because you haven't heard back from someone about taking a particular item. Start on another item.

Clutter

Clutter doesn't always mean we're talking about a room. Maybe it's an attic, a kitchen drawer, basement, a closet. It could even be a garage.

The issue is not where it is. The issue is what are you going to do with all those things?

I suggest you start with patience. Be kind to yourself. If it took years to get all that stuff in there, it could take a minute or two to get it out again.

My friend Susan Gardner, founder of the first "Buried in Treasure" group, is an expert in the art of reducing clutter and cherishing the things that mean the most. She says, "If nothing in the room demands immediate attention, pick a work area, and start with the closest corner. Decide what's to happen to all the stuff in that small corner."

The object of this exercise is to find a new home for these things. If they belong somewhere else in your home, get them there. Some items can be returned to the owner, others given away. Some may find value at a charity or family member's house. When you come back to that table or workbench the next time, you will have a cleared space to help you organize a different set of things.

My wife made it a point to empty one drawer. Once the drawer was empty, she had a place to put stuff that would go to one destination for someone else to use. When the drawer was full, all the contents of the drawer were taken to that destination at one time.

The drawer was ready for another cycle.

The same strategy can apply to a whole room. It may take some time to empty a room, but it really feels good to hit these milestone occasions. Congrats! You cleared a room.

By clearing a whole room, you've added to your strategy. Now you have a whole room to use as a staging area. That can help the rest of your project. Now you can put stuff for the thrift store in another corner. Corner two holds the stuff you're keeping—perhaps to review later. The third corner is for your favorite charity. Corner four has the stuff you are discarding. Some may go to recycle.

The rest of your discards are headed to the landfill. Keep landfill issues in mind and make this pile as small as possible. When you have accumulated a carload, it is time to make deliveries.

Duplicates and Extras

How many toasters did you get as wedding presents? For that matter, how many vases, cups, towel sets, serving trays, and on and on? And those are the obvious items. As we worked at it, we kept getting surprised. We often went to the attic, opened a mystery box, and found a duplicate of another downstairs.
What other items are hidden? Where are they hidden?

Junk drawers are a good target. They are often tucked away in places only infrequently visited. Places like bottom drawers in kitchen, bath, and dining room. Other drawers can be in the workbench in the garage. They all look vaguely like this.

> Decluttering is an act of kindness to yourself. Having less to take care of means more time for you!

Everybody has drawers like this. There are so many things in there you can't possibly know what's a duplicate.

Just off the top, I can spot three pairs of scissors, no less than six pocketknives, and three can openers.

Duplicates can also be hiding in workshops, medicine cabinets, garages, closets, and other cupboards.

I think checking for duplicates is what spring cleaning used to be about: Making sure that every drawer and all the items in it were not just cleaned but reviewed, as well. It felt good to put a new paper-liner in the drawer when you were done too. Repeat this strategy for every drawer, every shelf in every room.

I'm thinking that if we still did spring cleaning, we might have a lot less trouble with the downsizing business.

The real task is to calculate some kind of normal. How many chefs are normal?

In our house we often had meals where two potato peelers made sense because the crowd was large, and the cook often welcomed a helper or two.

In our new apartment we decided that we didn't need two potato peelers. If it took two people to prepare potatoes, only one is needed to do the peeling. The other could chop and dice or set the table.

How many knives do you really need? How many bottles of aspirin? Do you really need three sets of metric socket wrenches?

On the other hand, I also judged that we didn't need a battery powered drill. What kind of projects could I possibly have at the new place that would require a drill? Besides, at the new place, I could call on the maintenance staff to do any drill work.

Guess what? At latest count, there have been four times I regret that loss. Oh well, nothing is perfect. (After editing this, I realize that the last time I needed that drill was four months ago. Maybe getting rid of it was a good idea for the long haul.)

When you've lived in a house for 46 years, you know where things are.

When you move everything to different cabinets and drawers, you no longer have accurate patterns in your head for locating things.

Somebody, please tell me where the recipe book went. And Crys' set of password notes.

It is very hard to tell whether you forgot to take it with or it is just buried in a strange place.

Precious

What will you do with that art project your daughter did when she was six now that her son is in college?

If there is one thing we had enough of in our house, it is paper. Letters, reports, school papers, business papers, writings about the family, scrapbooks, and countless pictures, many depicting people we don't recognize. And, of course, there is nobody around to identify these strangers.

What do you do with all this stuff?

We asked our daughter to review her early artwork; she had no interest in keeping it. We photographed several pieces. We'll send the photos to her or family members at appropriate times. They're reminders that we've cherished her and her work for a very long time. And in the meantime, we can recycle the paper.

Earlier this year my wife and I published a book about us. We were given a subscription to StoryWorth a year earlier and started receiving and answering questions every week. What was your favorite sport when you were a kid? Were you ever in trouble at school? What was your hometown like? At the end of the year StoryWorth printed a book for us.

This project gave us the opportunity to use a lot of the old photos we had. Then, we were able to discard a great many scrapbooks and pictures.

We'll use this same process to capture other stories about our family and, of course, print the old photos we have of them in a new StoryWorth volume. The photos can then be discarded as well. In the meanwhile, we now have in our small storage area organized boxes of old photographs destined to become new volumes.

It's never too early to simplify your life. I know you will "probably live here forever," but you really can't predict when you may need to move. A job opportunity may surprise you. A sudden injury may force you to action. Retirement spurs many to move "closer to their grandkids."

A move may sneak up on you.

"Never happen!" says you. This summer we met with some friends that we'd not seen for 40 years. They recently had to move out of their house they'd been in for 26 years, and they had only three weeks to do it.

We also met a lady here in our retirement community who "got moved" from her home half-way across the country. Due to her failing health, her son wanted to be closer. He couldn't make the move. She could whether she wanted to or not.

In his book *Let It Go*, Peter Walsh looks at these "precious" items with a list of questions. He says a good goal is to "clear away stuff that doesn't represent who you are." He uses a series of questions to help make those decisions:

- Objects you never liked
- Things you regret having paid so much money to buy
- Stuff you inherited and hold on to out of a sense of obligation
- Outdated belongings that identify a version of you that vanished long ago[2]

Perhaps his questions can guide you, as well.

What Did We Learn?

Downsizing is not just a thing you have to do to get from one home to the next. Downsizing is also a way you can

1) Avoid unnecessary expense replacing items you already own,
2) Make space that you can really live in, and

3) Help avoid a big problem when you get the unexpected surprise of having to move.

Whether you are moving or not, there are definite benefits of having less. I take my cues from Joshua Becker, a noted minimalist. His website, becomingminimalist.com, is a treasure trove of details. Here are a couple of the benefits I found appealing.

When you have less you can

- Display what you value most
- Find things easier
- Have time for what matters the most
- Have less stress
- Spend less[3]

Give downsizing a try. What could you lose? Perhaps some old stuff you don't use anyway? Maybe some duplicates?

Start now.

Bonus Topic: When you've taken the seemingly endless pile of stuff to a new home, finally moved to your new place, and carefully unpacked all that great stuff, you'd think downsizing were done. It's not. As I'm writing this script, my wife just left to take a downsizing load to the thrift shop. Turns out we didn't have a use for those lamps, step stool, or towels in the new place.

When you are conscientious about your stuff and try to minimize, downsizing doesn't stop. Ever. The benefits from downsizing efforts live on, however.

> You can get rid of that if you hang on to the story it represents.

PART 2

Where Did It All Go?

5 OUR RULES FOR DOWNSIZING

My wife Crys and I just moved. In the process, we had to downsize. In this section I want to talk about where all that stuff went and just how you might downsize without upsizing the landfill.

A great deal of it went with us. We decided that we still needed the chairs, rug, waste cans, and Christmas tree, and, as the picture shows, all those boxes.

But what about all the rest? We moved from a 1660 square foot house. Oh, yes, it also had a nearly full attic.

We went from almost 3300 square feet to our new 1130 square foot apartment. Not everything we owned was going to fit in the smaller space.

Let's now talk about where all that stuff went. Here is my list of just how many things left the house. Settle back. Getting through this list will take a little time.

Our possessions went to a variety of homes, charities, companies, friends, churches and more. In fact, by the day we moved in we had taken 170 sets of things out of our house. Each set represented one place or destination for this trip. The last five items on the list we took out of our apartment after the move. We've been downsizing or, as my friend would say, right-sizing to fit our new home and life.

The variety is incredible. One page of the list alone included a hammered dulcimer and clarinet, toys, a variety of bird feeders, and a small telescope. A second page detailed shirts, gloves, puzzles, a collection of Santa Claus figurines from around the world.

Then there was the stuff we found under the deck and in our tool shed like small rolls of fencing.

And from the dining room we discovered multiple tablecloths, decorator plates, and specialty towels. It amazed us to find countless things hiding in plain sight.

Who knew that we had an inherited collection of antique Bibles from the 1800's? Add to that wooden toys, napkin rings, treadmill, folding chairs, small tables, and on and on.

I invite you to walk through your house. I bet you will also find a wide variety of things. It's amazing the kinds of things you accumulate when you live in the same house for 46 years! I'm thinking there are way too many items to show here. Let's divide them into some smaller categories.

But first, I want to talk about rules. Crys and I had three rules to guide our rightsizing efforts.

Rule #1: Obviously, we had to get rid of stuff. The only things we stored were two furniture pieces that matched our dining room set. They ended up in my daughter's house quite possibly for sale later.

Rule #2: We really, really did not want to just throw things away. Why?

The stuff you and I throw out goes to the landfill and we did not want to contribute to that mound of waste. The sooner we fill up a pile like the one in the picture, the sooner our city will have to find another piece of property to use. The more you and I put in the landfill, the higher the likelihood that you and I will contribute to polluting our air and water supply. I know I don't want to do that, and I believe you don't either. Besides, who wants to live near this kind of thing? We didn't want to contribute to global warming or environmental injustice.

Our Rules for Downsizing

Rule #3: See if we could find a home for our stuff where it could be cherished.

Kitten anyone? Allergies or not, I've cherished many kittens in my life. Wouldn't it be great if everything you and I try to get rid of had as good a chance to find a home as does a fluffy, cute kitten? Cuteness makes up for a lot. Sadly, not everything is cute.

I suggest you categorize items based on the value they have. We have three categories. Obviously, some things are more valued than others. We'll start with the lowest rung on the value ladder:

1. Stuff nobody wants.

What comes next is "Stuff people want." We'll divide that group in half:

2. Things others could find homes for, like thrift shops, and
3. Stuff for which we found owners who would cherish them.

6 STUFF NOBODY WANTS

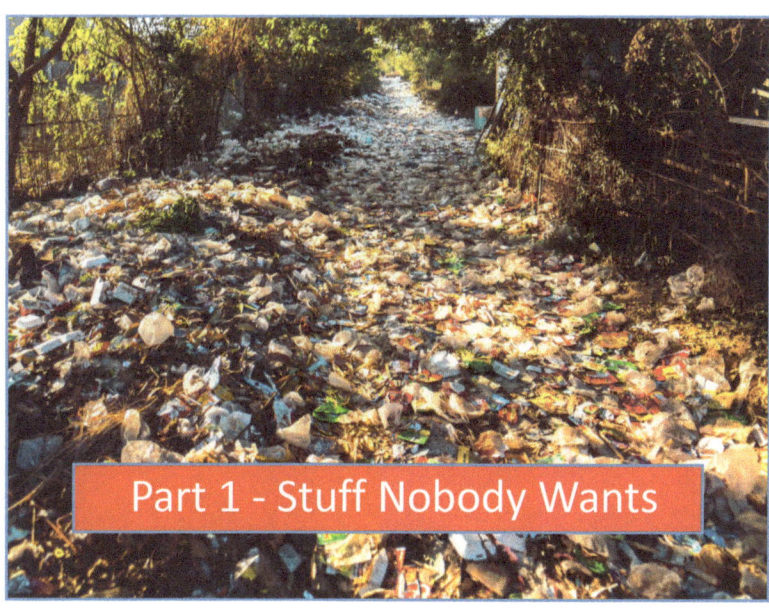

Stuff like this is commonly known as trash. The hard thing about trash is, that we don't want it to end up in the landfill. So, where can it go?

It is a lot harder to get rid of these things than it would be to find a home for some cherished possession.

There are a lot of candidates in that category. How about Styrofoam? Do you want Styrofoam around?

My wife and I occasionally received a box filled with something we had ordered or brought home from the store. Look around the room. Which of the items you see came in a box?

- Furniture
- Electronics
- Washing machine
- TV
- Tables
- Lamps

Inside these boxes you could always find packing material—often hard Styrofoam. Not the peanut stuff; that's soft Styrofoam. We kept the boxes and the hard Styrofoam just in case. If we wanted to get rid of that TV, we'd have the box and packing material that fit.

Guess what we found in the attic? All kinds of boxes that, once upon a time, held valuable household items. Sadly, we'd gotten rid of the items but were left with the boxes and the Styrofoam. We can put the cardboard in our city's recycle bin, but what do you do with Styrofoam was a problem? Our solution was a place we found called Engineered Foam Packaging.

What does Engineered Foam Packaging (EFP) do? Well, it takes that hard Styrofoam like ours in at one end of the building and out the other end comes, reconstituted Styrofoam. You heard me right. They turn Styrofoam into Styrofoam.

Your Styrofoam comes in their front door. EFP processes it and sends it out the back door in response to the requests from companies that need Styrofoam to build those packages like the packages you started out with.

This Styrofoam we gave EFP will eventually end up in the landfill. But at least we kept it in circulation where it was working and stopped other people from making as much brand-new Styrofoam. Not quite as good a care of nature as I'd like, but hey, it beats tossing it into landfill to start with.

What else? Techno trash. Now, what does techno trash include? We had a cabinet in our house that had drawers filled with VCR tapes, CDs and DVDs. Anybody out there have similar supplies? Yes, we had VCR tapes long after we had a VCR player to put them on. What do you do with that stuff? The place we sent it to is called GreenDisk.

GreenDisk is a pay-for service. They won't dispose of your stuff for free, but they will take it and send it off and responsibly reuse it or destroy it so it doesn't necessarily end up in the landfill. Green Disk is scalable; they also have containers that can work in your office.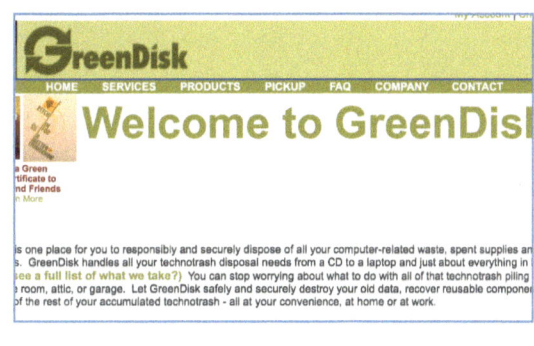

Don't forget local recycling. In our case, our city has built several centers around town where you can take hard to get rid of things like batteries or tires, mattresses, or fluorescent light bulbs. Every kind of battery from the tiniest to the car battery can go there. They'll also

take oil-based paint. If you are like us, you might have a whole row of paint cans in the attic because you had a gray house and then you had a green house.

Local organizations often host "recycle" or "green" days where special items can be disposed of. The Tennessee Environmental Council hosts an event where we were able to rid ourselves of chicken-wire fencing, an old mailbox, sections of downspout, cables and assorted gear, and odds and ends of yard tools we'd collected over the years.

Did you know that in Nashville, at least, latex-based paint can be put in the standard brown curb-side bins, the landfill bins?

You must dry it first, however. They won't take liquid paint. You have a choice. You can open the cans and let the paint dry naturally or you can fill those cans with cat litter. Either method means you can eventually dispose of latex paint safely. I don't recall exactly, but I believe the cat litter did the job in about a month. The natural drying method would have taken much, much longer.

You can use specially designated drop off places for oil-based paint or fluorescent lightbulbs, tires or mattresses, bleach or antifreeze, and a host of other things. Not all these items leach into the ground water, but many of them do. Anybody care for a nice refreshing glass of antifreeze? There is a good reason for why much of this stuff is classified as hazardous waste.

Take care. Regulations for hazardous waste disposal vary by locality.

Surprisingly, two places in Nashville will take paint itself. ReStore, sponsored by Habitat for Humanity will take unopened latex-based cans of paint. Turnip Green Creative Reuse will take partial cans of paint. More about Turnip Green later.

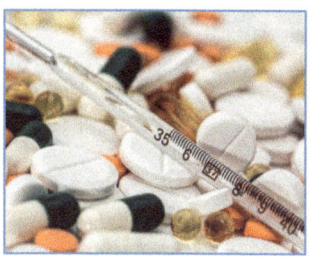

Another item hard to dispose of is drugs. You don't want various concoctions of medicinals leaching into the ground water or stuck on a trash pile for someone with a craving to find. It is also not safe to dispose of these items in the sink or toilet only to end up in local rivers and streams or our drinking water.

In our area police departments dispose of these items. Likewise, the fire department stations often will see that these things get destroyed in a non-hazardous way.

Last, but not least, what do you do with all those containers you keep around? You know, the plastic boxes and bottles.

We have a community garden in Nashville. People come and take fruits and vegetables as well as flowers. They sometimes need containers for their customers to use the haul off their produce.

Sage Refill Market stores bulk items and lets you "refill" your container. For example, you can get hand soap and laundry soap and more. They can almost always use your extra empty bottles for their customers who didn't bring enough containers.

You know how this works:

Let's just repeat the idea for everyday household items.

Refill please!

7 STUFF SOMEBODY IS BOUND TO WANT

Part 2 - Somebody Wants These Things

That takes us to a second category: items that might be cherished by someone else.

There are really two brands of cherished items. The first set includes things that still have value. They should not be thrown out. If you just can't find who might be interested, there are organizations who specialize in finding new homes for things. The difference between finding a new owner often has to do with quantity.

You might find a home for some pencils, but not for all the old school supplies that you'll not need any longer.

What you need is some kind of broker who will find the homes you don't have time to find.

Let's start with those things that seem to accumulate in the dark, in the closet, in drawers. The list includes printing paper that fit the old printer but not the current one, old boxes, pens, erasers pencils, and shipping envelopes of various sizes.

We all have accumulated a lifetime supply of perfectly usable and once important stuff that we just don't need anymore. What do you do with all that?

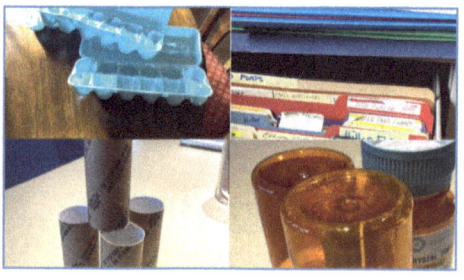

Don't forget paint, fabric, candles, party supplies, ribbons, flower arranging foam pieces, sewing supplies, party supplies, paper plates and cups, egg cartons, chopsticks, left-over flooring tiles, floral arrangements, pictures, toilet paper rolls, and pill bottles.

There is an organization in Nashville called Turnip Green Creative Reuse. It's not recycling; it is Reuse: giving things a new purpose. If you are an artisan, a teacher, a Cub Scout leader, or just curious, you would go to Turnip Green Creative Reuse and get supplies.

When you approach Turnip Green's facility, you wonder whether you've happened upon a neatly organized annex to the Metro Nashville landfill. But believe me—people use Turnip Green a lot because where you might just see junk you have lying around the house, they can envision some exciting different treasure.

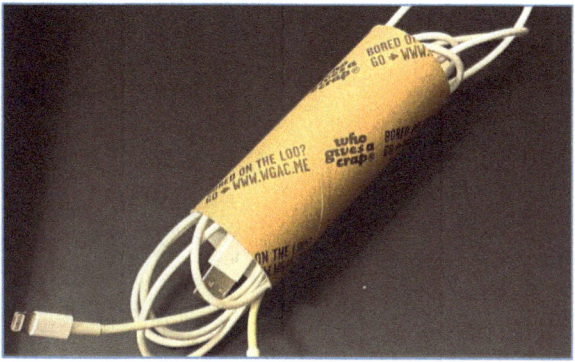

There may be ways to reuse some of this stuff: a toilet paper roll is a convenient place to put cables. But... I have many more toilet paper rolls than I do cables. Turnip Green is the place where my toilet paper rolls can wait for someone to show up who has more uses for them than I.

School teachers find classroom decorations, art and crafts supplies, and organizational aids. Craft people from all over come by to see what they can find to make their next masterpiece. They are searching through things no longer of value to you that are still usable and of value to them.

A local place called Junkdrop Nashville offers home clean-outs. They partner with other organizations like Habitat and Goodwill Industries to find homes for appliances, clothes, and the like. Similarly, Tri-Start Recycling will take surplus electronics to needed users in schools, hospitals, and more. A search on the web can be of great help as you hunt for people who will find new homes for what is no longer needed in your home.

Another whole category of items went to various thrift shops in the area. Often connected to church or synagogue ministries, thrift shops specialize in resale of your used items. For example, we made 17 trips to places like these and took clothes, lamps, books, suitcases, and more.

One special place we found is called McKay's. It specializes in buying books and electronics you don't want and providing a retail outlet where people can come and shop for their next treasure. Billed as a "used bookstore," McKay's is a great place to take things that can be re-used. Got a DVD movie you've seen and want to get a different one? How about a sci fi book or romance novel? Need a place for a digital camera or old phone?

McKay's will take all these things and either pay you cash or give you in-store credit. If you don't want to use the in-store credit and buy more books or videos for yourself, give the voucher to some kind of literacy program, preschool, or "Little Free Library" near you.

Besides McKay's we also donated books to various private collections. Religious books and our family's collection of old Bibles went to our church, popular novels went to our retirement community, a gardening for birds book went to a neighbor.

Did we get rid of everything? Hardly. After purging our Christmas decorations, we kept these little angels among other things. They are antique and came from my wife's mom. Will we keep them forever?  Probably not. But they have been on a windowsill or mantel at Christmas time for decades. So, as my daughter says, "Keep them around for a while.

Maybe next Christmas you'll have more clarity about where they should go."

As I write this, we haven't had Christmas in our new place yet; I'm curious as to whether we'll decide to keep these among the Christmas ornaments for next year.

The point is some things might be hard to let go of. So, don't. Find a way to circle back around later and decide then.

The second largest set of things we got rid of went to an entrepreneurial young man named Paul who specializes in helping folks like us make a move. Under the company name Moving Help, Paul buys and then sells the things you don't want. Ironically, Paul has the same problem we did—he can't afford to pay to store things. Consequently, he works fast.

Paul came to visit one day to take a few more pictures. After he left, we got in the car and took off for errands. We drove right by Paul who was sitting in his car parked at the curb madly working on his phone. I confirmed with him later that he was posting his latest pictures on a sales site of some sort.

All together Paul took an ottoman, four stuffed chairs, and three couches that we knew would not fit in our new apartment. He also took a treadmill, two bar stools with small circular table to match, a largely unused juicer, a set of flatware, some porch furniture, steel folding chairs, two small and narrow tables, plus cushions.

The best part about his taking these items was that we didn't have to pay for transport or figure out where all this stuff should go. Ten days before we moved, Paul called to check on availability. He showed up with a friend on that Saturday, took two couches to the driveway. A half hour later, two of his buyers came and hauled off their new acquisitions. Bonus for Paul!

We didn't have to find buyers or lug furniture. Yippee! And Paul didn't have to transport or store these items either.

If you are looking for that kind of functionality, I hope you find your "Paul." I also understand that there are several non-profit organizations that will pick up furniture donations.

As you may recall, my mom made use of a person specializing in estate sales. I understood that she asked several of her friends to move her to an apartment. Once done, what was left was handled by the estate salesperson. He ferreted out the "good stuff" to get to buyers he'd done business with before. He counted on a public auction, "estate sale," to get rid of the rest. As I've written before, mom got rid of 50 years' worth of treasures in ONE day.

This estate sale model is a good way of getting household goods to a new set of owners in a short period of time. Some people use garage sales for the same reason. We chose not to do that. We didn't want to drag everything out of the house, price it, sell it for pennies on the dollar, and turn around to carry half of it back into the house.

> You are not only downsizing your house, but also your worries.

8 STUFF SOMEBODY TOOK GLADLY

For many items, we found homes, homes where having the item made a difference. We were very thoughtful about friends and neighbors. Who among them would want what? For example…

Friends and Neighbors Can Help

One very good friend of ours teaches photography at a local college. She values old photos. We raided the attic for her and pulled out all those photo books we inherited from various sets of parents and grandparents and found an incredible number of pictures of people we didn't know and places we'd never been. Off to university they went. Turnip Green will take these photos too for many of the same reasons.

I ran a tech sale early on to get rid of odds and ends of equipment once important to me but were of better use to others. A headset with mic anyone?

What collections have you cherished over the years. Baseball cards? Coins? Stamps?

If you look carefully, you can find places to get rid of coin collections and stamp collections and green depression ware and silver. It takes time. One of the reasons we started early on was because we didn't know where this stuff was going to go. It's going to take time to find just the right place.

A neighbor of ours was an avid stamp collector. He got several stamp books and small boxes of loose stamps that Crys created 65+ years ago.

A friend mentioned that her teenage boys loved throwing darts. I dug out several sets that I used regularly once upon a time, and they found a new home. We recently had dinner with these folks; they were delighted with their new darts.

In the sports category, what do you have hidden away in closets? How about golf clubs, tennis or badminton rackets, lawn darts, and croquet sets?

Many bicycle shops collect bicycles. They often refurbish them and donate them to people who need basic transportation. We posted the availability of our two bikes on a neighborhood list serve and sold them in less than an hour.

Long ago in our first home in California, I started collecting tools. It was wonderful to be able to use the magnificent solid-steel workbench the previous owner had built. For the first time I didn't have to borrow tools just to fix something. Many of those tools moved with us to Nashville 50 years ago. Sadly, I had to leave the steel table behind. It was much too heavy to transport.

Four years after the move to Nashville we bought a home complete with carport and shed. The first thing I did in the shed was to build a work bench. When we built the deck, the shed came down and the work bench went away. Over the years I repaired fewer and fewer things requiring fewer and fewer tools. And finally, when we prepared for the coming move, I was down to a toolbox and four or five storage bins for tools and odds and ends like screws. connectors, wires, and so forth. When we moved to this retirement community, I gave most of the remainder to a good friend who is into fixing things. FYI: I'm down to one drawer with tools.

Our "adopted" granddaughters next door inherited a whole set of children's toys.

The neighborhood list serve also came in handy to get rid of two harmonicas and two flutes for a music program the young man was involved in. Other neighbors got books about gardening, my father-in-law's rock collection, a telescope, a baby doll cradle, a set of robot toys.

Family Can Help

I solicited a blog post some time ago from Rhonda Smart who, at the time, did estate sales. She remarked that some items once thought valuable but have less value in today's world.

Our kids don't even want them.

For example: Where do we put the silver my wife inherited? It's going for very low prices even on eBay.

My wife had been gifted or inherited, count them, four separate sets of flatware, three of which were in those beautiful hardwood boxes. We do a lot of entertaining, but we don't do that much entertaining.

What can you do with those sets? My daughter got one set, we took one set, but the others went to refugee resettlement. When people come in this country, they come often without anything. When people are setting up an apartment, they need things like silverware. So those were welcome additions for them. From the reports we got, the families were delighted.

Early on during our downsizing effort, my daughter came over and went through the collection of items we were trying to part with. Crys and I thought sure she would be interested in many things.

She was. And, my son-in-law got the gas grill and cover along with all the grilling paraphernalia.

But it turned out that a whole list of items we thought would appeal to her did not. Equally surprising, she was interested in some things we had no idea she had her eye on. Let's review a couple of items that her family now values.

Here is a picture of my wife's inherited grandfather's clock. It is so old, that we refer to it as my wife's grandfather's, grandfather's, grandfather's clock.

We had to have a clock-smith dismantle this and put it back together at my daughter's house.

This clock has literally been handed down generation after generation from the late 1700s. As the oldest of all the grandchildren, Crys inherited it when her grandfather died.

Another thing we had a lot of accumulation of was green depression glass tableware. Our starter set was a wedding gift from Crys' other grandmother. We bought more, and people would bring us serving pieces and other things as gifts. We ended up with a huge collection. Some went to my daughter. She wanted the serving pieces. But surprise, she didn't want the matching place settings.

We found a home for those place settings with a family who visited us at holiday time and had dinner using our collection of depression glass. She  liked it a lot and took the rest so that she could do dinners at her house. I'm glad to say in both cases—with our daughter and our friend—we have visiting rights. We can go see our stuff. After all, we used those place settings a lot and will miss them particularly at holiday time.

My wife inherited a lot of very precious, hand-made, and antique doilies and tablecloths that were passed down from one generation to the next in hope chests and the like. We found little interest in our family and friends to keep them.

Out of curiosity, I looked these up on the internet this morning and found very inexpensive knock offs. These retail pieces probably didn't have any of those pesky missed stitches and the like that usually travel with hand-made goods. Nor do they capture the love and planning that went into each stitch.

My daughter wasn't interested in keeping her child-hood works of art. Turns out she didn't want to keep much of her son's artwork either!

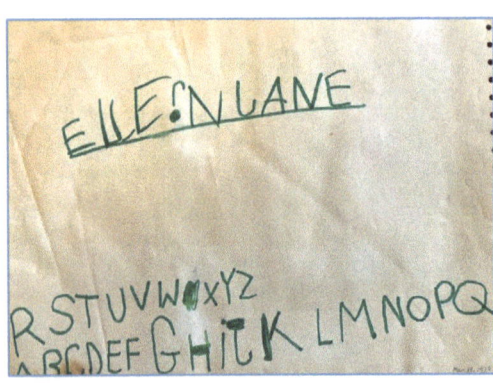

Come on. Isn't this worth passing on? Well, we did. We're not quite sure yet, but we're planning on making another StoryWorth book or two to hold the digital images we've collected.

The moral of the story is that it might take some time to find homes for some cherished items. But you will be deeply satisfied to know your treasures will be treasured again by someone else!

9 USEFUL GUIDELINES

Looking back over our moving experience, here are some useful guidelines.

Allow Time

Be easy on yourself, allow enough time. It took years to collect all that stuff. It will take time to find everything a new home. This is particularly true if you really want to achieve the goals we laid out.

You can limit the time you spend doing this to weekends if you like. Just remember: It will take MANY weekends. Very early on, we allocated a day a week trying to get rid of stuff. We spent the other days isolating collections and pulling car loads together. The allocated day was often used to make multiple trips for different collections.

I'm not sure, but I believe the time you'll need depends on how much space you've allocated for your possessions and how many years you've stayed in one dwelling.

Each effort has limits, however. After sifting and sorting and deciding, my brain got tired. The experts call this decision-overload. I had to mix in some other activities and save more decision-making for another day.

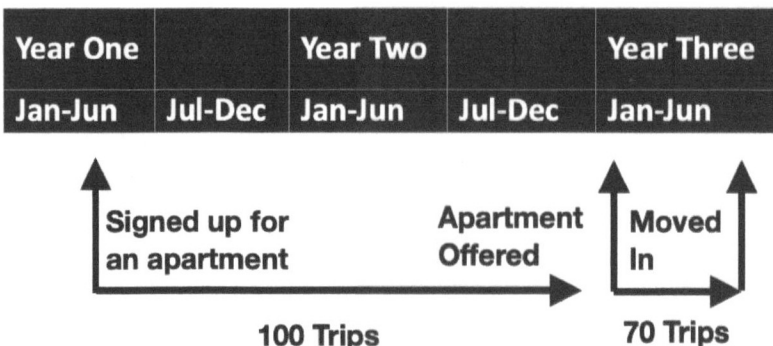

To give you some idea of how long it took us, we were told we had four to five years to wait before there would be an apartment available in our chosen retirement community. We did start downsizing immediately, however. A little over a year and a half later we were surprised with an offer for an apartment, and we decided to move ahead. At that point we had taken 100 sets of things out of the house. Each set was a line item on the spreadsheet I showed you earlier.

We moved almost two years after the decision was made. By that time, we had taken 170 trips of stuff out of our house. From the perspective of the house, this last trip, taking the stuff we were to keep, the actual move was the biggest downsizing effort of all. We were home!

Again.

Start Now

One secret for success is nearly hidden in the sequence: We didn't wait to get started, and we didn't begin with the stuff most precious to us.

You don't have to wait or let go of cherished items immediately. Go ahead. Hit that junk drawer. Find out what those mystery boxes are in the attic or basement. It all has to go. Start on the stuff that matters least to you. Get going now. It was well over a year into our effort before a family friend noticed that stuff was disappearing from the more frequented public-facing rooms.

Team Effort

We also concluded that all this downsizing and moving must be a team effort.

I already mentioned how valuable our daughter's help was. She went through and decided what she would like to have for the long term. We could cross a lot of things off the list because they're spoken for. She was very good about pointing out options and offering grace: "No," she would say, "you can keep that around if you're unsure and decide about it later." Oh, yes, she also helped with the space planning.

There could be other people you might involve. We talked about Paul, the young man who spoke up for a lot of items, paid us for them, and took care of hauling them off. This was valuable to us as he took off some of the heaviest of items: the treadmill, hide-a-bed, and couches. Other people who needed to downsize have relied on estate sale companies or consignment shops.

We also hired a moving company that did more than just haul off boxes. They helped with planning and then…

- Day 1: Three nice people from the company did all the packing.

- Day 2: Three hefty guys hauled away all the stuff and put it in the apartment where it belonged according to our plans.

- Day 3: Two nice people from the moving company took much of the stuff out of the boxes and put it back where it belonged, even re-stocked the refrigerator.

- Day 4: Drapes were hung, final boxes were unpacked, and the bed made. We could straighten drawer contents and go to lunch in our new home!

Bing, bang, boom… we were there. We stayed at our daughter's for two nights, days 2 and 3 of the move. On the fourth day of the move we slept in our own bed at the new place.

That nice company was Let's Get Moving. They provided excellent service and filled an important niche in our moving and downsizing effort. I'm sure you could find similar services outside of our hometown of Nashville, Tennessee.

You can also let your friends or neighbors or colleagues do some of the deciding. Take a page out of Crys' aunt's playbook: Put some items out for guests and family. Let them take home the things they always valued. Or, as we mentioned, get the word out to neighbors using local newspapers or emails to groups.

Date	Destination	Items
8/29/22	Recycle	Half a recycle tub of old card/boxes
10/13/22	Open Table	Sleeping bag, 2 blankets, ear muffs, gloves
10/13/22	Room in the Inn	Shirts, sweater, vest, sweat pants &
10/15/22	E-waste	Electonics
10/15/22		…nders, heavy duty …lored paper,
10/15/22	GoodWill	Shirts, gloves, knife
10/15/22	Police	Old Rx & vet meds

Keep Track

Have you ever gone to the garage to find something you just knew was there only to not be able to find it?

When we started this project, I started cataloging what left when. That's my third tip; make a list. Next week when I complain, "I thought we had one of those." I can check the list. This very thing happened to me the second day after we moved in. Boy, was I disappointed that the little electric drill was on the list and not in my reduced tool drawer.

The list also reminds us of what we've done. Progress is always a good motivator.

Let Go

Then there is the biggest trick of all: Letting go. Having less stuff around does mean, as our friend would say, "Less to dust." Having less stuff also means less clutter, less dependence on things. BONUS!

To be sure, you can't live without some things. But how much do you need? After all, fewer things also means less to worry about.

Since we followed our son-in-law's advice about thinking through what our lifestyle included and then went to all the trouble to plan how different elements of the apartment fit into those styles, we were eager to move. We had something to look forward to. It wasn't just a loss. It was a new beginning and yet familiar. It was home.

We also found that it is easier to let go if you focus on where it will go to do some good.

As Joshua Becker, the minimalist guy, says, "Moving to less might just be a spiritual journey." [4]

Before I leave, I've one parting question:

What's in your attic?

I challenge you. Look around. What should go now? What can go now? If you want to live better with less stress, start now.

FOOTNOTES AND CREDITS

1. *Keep the Memories, Lose the Stuff*, by Matt Paxton with Jordan Michael Smith, Penguin, Copyright © 2022 by Matt Paxton

2. *Let It Go: Downsizing Your Way to a Richer, Happier Life*, by Peter Walsh, Rodale, an imprint of Random House. Copyright © 2017 by Peter Walsh

3. *Benefits of Minimalism: 21 Benefits of Owning Less*, a blog post at Becomingminimalist.com. Copyright © 2023 by Joshua Becker

4. *Things That Matter: Overcoming Distraction to Pursue a More Meaningful Life*, by Joshua Becker with Eric Stanford. Waterbrook, an imprint of Random House, Copyright © 2022 by Becoming Minimalist, LLC. Becker has several other books and YouTube channels.

Most pictures were supplied by the author. Commercial photographs were supplied under subscription to unsplash.com and pexels.com.

Join Ed on his website for other exciting resources:

retirementkickstart.com